STAY OPTIMISTIC EVERY DAY!

Birister Sharma

Copyright © 2022 Birister Sharma

All Rights Reserved.

Made with ❤on the Notion Press Platform

www.notionpress.com

Dedicated to my loving wife....

Pallabi Devi Sharma

I surrendered to you, O my Lord......

"Om Namah Shivaya"

Table of Contents

One word

Be optimistic in your life. Without optimism, you can't live your life. It is only your optimism that leads you even in the darkness of your life. It is only your optimism that shows you the silver lining in the dark clouds.

If you are optimistic, it means you know yourself.

If you are optimistic, it means you love yourself.

If you are optimistic, it means you are positive in your life.

If you are optimistic, it means you believe in yourself.

If you are optimistic, it means you have self-confidence.

If you are optimistic, it means you know your goal.

If you are optimistic, it means you have a purpose in your life.

Only an optimistic person can live in this world. Only an optimistic person can enjoy his life fully, even in the midst of sorrows and hardships.

An optimistic person sees possibility in every calamity. But a pessimistic person sees the impossible in every golden opportunity.

1. Be Happy

Always decide to make yourself happy.

Make yourself happy. Your happiness is always yours. If you are not happy with yourself, then nobody in the entire world will make you happy. Your happiness is decided by you, not by anyone else. Life is yours, as is your happiness. You are the owner of your own happiness. It is your own asset. Only you can manage your happiness.

It is up to you how you can make yourself happy. There is no role for anyone else. You have to play your own role. You have to seek your own happiness. You have to discover your own happiness. You will never receive your happiness from an external source. You will only receive your happiness from the internal source that is within yourself.

Grow your own happiness.

Your world is like a garden, and you are its gardener. It depends on you what type of plants and what variety of flowers you would like to grow in your garden. It also depends on you how you look after your garden. In fact, everything depends on you. In the same fashion, your happiness is like the plants and the flowers that you grow and nurture in the garden of your life.

You are the host of your own happiness.

You are the best host of your own happiness. Your happiness is just like your guest. It always depends on you how you greet it. If you greet it with your love, respect, and compassion, then it will always stay with you like your beloved ones; but unfortunately, if you ever treat it badly and harshly, it will leave you forever. It will never come back to you.

Always open the door to your happiness

Never close the door of your happiness; otherwise, it will always lock up your happiness. Don't make enmity with your happiness; make friendship with it. It will always hold your life and world together. Your happiness is your greatest energy and power. It will boost and cherish your life. Always keep the door of your mind, heart, and soul open so that the fresh winds of happiness will blow into your life forever.

You are the master of your own happiness.

If you decide to be happy, then nobody can make you unhappy without your consent. You are the lord of your own happiness. Build the castle of your own happiness. Rule over it. But never allow the intruder of your happiness to enter it. Guard it like a vigilant gatekeeper, day in and day out.

In a small town, two men are living. One is Mr. Happy, and the other is Mr. Unhappy.Mr. Happy is always happy. He wakes up early in the morning every day. He is active in every activity. He regularly goes to his office on time. He loves his job, even though his position is the lowest rank. He sets his goals every day. He is a disciplined man. He is positive. He is optimistic in his life. He gets enough time to spend quality time with his family members. His life is happy and prosperous.

On the other hand, Mr. Unhappy is never happy even though he has a superior position in his office. He wakes up late in the morning every day. He is inactive in every activity. He is irregular at his office. He hates his job. He has no goals in his life. He is an undisciplined man. He is negative. He is pessimistic in his life. He seldom spends quality time with his family members. His life is unhappy and mediocre.

From the natures of the above two men, how could we sum up?

We always find two kinds of people around us: one is Mr. Happy, who is always happy and optimistic, and the other is Mr. Unhappy, who is always unhappy and pessimistic.

Mr. Happy is always happy because he decides to be happy. He has many reasons to make himself happy. Mr. Unhappy has always been unhappy because he decides to be unhappy. He has no reason to make himself happy.

When you decide to be happy, your positivity, punctuality, discipline, optimism, and prosperity will automatically follow you. Your life will settle and become organized. On the contrary, when you decide to be unhappy, everything turns against you. Everything turns upside down. Unsettled and disorganized.

You have to decide for yourself what you want to become in your life: like Mr. Happy or like Mr. Unhappy.

In your life, always decide to be like Mr. Happy. Never decide to be like Mr. Unhappy.

A happy man is always optimistic in his life; an unhappy man is always pessimistic. A happy man never complains about anything; he accepts everything gladly. He is satisfied with himself. But an unhappy man always complains about everything, even when he has abundance in his life. He never accepts anything. He is disturbed by himself.

A happy man always wants to see everybody happy. On the other hand, an unhappy man never wants to see anyone happy.

Always decide to be happy in your life, no matter what happens.

If you decide to be happy, then nobody can make you unhappy without your consent.

You are the maker of your own happiness.

2. Expect the Best

The best things will only happen in your life when you expect
the best things.

In a small village, a poor farmer was living with his family. He
owned a small piece of agricultural land that was not fertile,
inherited from his ancestors. He worked very hard, but he produced
very small amounts of grain, which were not sufficient for his family.
However, the poor farmer was always optimistic in his life and
always expected the best things to happen. So, he devoted himself to
his work in the best possible way without making any complaints.
Many of his friends advised him to go to the town for work rather
than depend on his small, infertile land. The poor farmer didn't heed
his friends' advice and worked hard, tirelessly, and constantly with
his complete dedication.

Then, one day, the poor farmer decided to grow cash crops
along with the regular food crops. When he was ploughing the land
with his two old oxen, all of a sudden, the plough plank hit against
something very hard. He halted his ploughing and started digging at
the place where the plough plank hit. After digging for a while, he
found a rusted old casket. He took out the casket and opened its lock.
When he opened the casket, he stumbled and was tongue-tied. The
rusted old casket was full of gold coins. He thanked Almighty God
with heartfelt gratitude. His best expectations paid him a huge
amount of wealth, enough for his next seven generations.

In the early phase of our lives, we are all like poor farmers. Life
throws many tough challenges and upheavals upon us. But we
shouldn't give up; we should accept everything with open arms. We
have to expect the best and work towards our goals with full
dedication and conviction. Who knows when the casket of great
fortune will knock at our feet?

You have to listen to your heart and follow your own intuition. No matter how many countless challenges and upheavals strike in your life, you must stick to your single-minded goal. Forget every secondary and unnecessary thing. Eventually, you will witness the best moment in your life.

When you firmly stand by your commitments and focus on your aims and objectives, you will definitely succeed in your life. Nobody will dare to stop you. You will be able to tackle every hurdle in your life easily. And lady luck will be bound to please you with your hard work and dedication.

When you expect the best things in your life, you will receive the best things in your life. Your life will respond to you the way you expect. But if you expect the worst things in your life, you will receive the worst things in your life.

When you expect something in your life, your mind, heart, and soul will start following your command and try to fulfill your expectations at any cost. It doesn't differentiate between anything, whether the best thing or the worst thing. Its only job is to fulfill your expectations.

If you command yourself to do great things in your life, you will surely start doing great things. But if you command yourself to do nothing in your life, you will surely do nothing.

When you expect the best things in your life, you will do the best things, and you will get the best things.

If you expect the best relationship in your life, you will really get the best relationship.

If you expect the best house in your life, then you will really build the best house.

If you expect the best work in your life, then you will really get the best work.

If you expect the best car in your life, then you will really own the best car.

If you expect the best comfort in your life, then you will really enjoy the best comfort.

If you expect the best outfit in your life, then you will really wear the best outfit.

If you expect the best result in your life, then you will really witness the best result.

If you expect the best life for yourself, then you will really live your best life.

Your best expectations have the power to fulfill everything for you because they are interconnected to your mind, heart, and soul. Your best expectations imply your strong desires to fulfill your aims, objectives, goals, and missions in life. Once you affirm yourself to turn your expectations into realities, then nobody can stop you. You will be guided by your expectations. You are bound to achieve your desired aims, objectives, goals, and missions.

The best things always follow the best things. The worst things always follow the worst things. This is the law of this universe. Everything depends on cause and effect. If the cause is the best, then its effects will definitely be the best.

Your expectations are like raw materials. If the raw materials of your expectations are the best, then the products of your expectations are always the best. If the raw materials of your expectations are the worst, then obviously the products of your expectations are always the worst.

The best raw material always produces the best product, and the worst raw material always produces the worst product.

What do you want in your life?

The best product or the worst product? You have to decide for yourself.

Nobody wants to become the worst in his or her life. And nobody wants to see the worst thing happen in his or her life.

Everybody wants to become the best in his or her life. Everybody wants to see the best thing happen in his or her life.

Never expect anything worse in your life. Always expect the best thing in your life. You are born to receive the best things in your life. But you are not born to receive the worst things in your life.

What about you? Ask yourself!

Always expect the best, and always achieve the best.

The way you expect, the way you think, the way you act, and the way you become in your life.

The best product of your life is only produced by your best expectations.

3. Trust the Universe

Nobody wants to become the worst in his or her life. And nobody wants to see the worst thing happen in his or her life.

Everybody wants to become the best in his or her life. Everybody wants to see the best thing happen in his or her life.

Never expect anything worse in your life. Always expect the best thing in your life. You are born to receive the best thing in your life. But you are not born to receive the worst thing in your life.

What about you? Ask yourself!

Always expect the best, and always achieve the best.

The way you expect, the way you think, the way you act, and the way you become in your life.

The best product of your life is only produced by your best expectations.

Trust is your life, and trust is your universe. Without trust, you can't live your life. Your trust is the foundation of your life.

This universe never does anything biased to you or to anyone. It is ever ready to help you. It is ever ready to guide you. But it depends on you whether you ask for help from it or not; whether you ask for guidance from it or not.

If you search for good things, you will get good things. If you search for success, you will get your success. If you search for victory, you will get your victory. Everything is available for you. No doubt, you will have to wait for some time, but this universe will bestow your desired result at the end when the right time comes. It may delay, but it will never deny. You have to keep your patience and hope alive.

You can discover everything in this universe. It is the law of this universe that you will get whatever you want, desire, and wish for. But there is only one condition: you have to trust yourself and trust this universe, and work for it with full dedication and conviction.

A scientist couldn't discover anything if he doesn't trust himself. He trusts himself because he trusts this universe. He knows that the things he will discover are available in this universe.

You are born to live; you are born to win; and you are born to be successful in your life. You have every reason to live in this universe. Never doubt yourself. Trust yourself and trust this universe. Make friends with yourself and make friends with this universe. This universe is your true friend. It will help you at every juncture of your life. It will never betray you.

No doubt, you will have to face the challenges of this universe. This is the reality of this universe. You have to accept it. You should never expect anything for free. You have to pay for everything. Before you gain something, you have to endure some pain. You have to sacrifice something in order to get something in return.

This universe is just like a huge ocean. It is abundant with treasures. If you want to accumulate these treasures in your life, then you have to dive into its deep core.

Nothing goes unrewarded in this universe. You will get your reward the way you want. You decide your own reward. For instance, if you grow a fruit plant, you will always relish its delicious juice. But if you grow a thorny bush, you will always get pricked by its thorns. The way you sow in your life is the way you reap in your life.

This whole universe is waiting for you for your great works, great achievements, and great contributions.

If you trust this universe, it will always be ready to help you wholeheartedly. You have to ask it. The more you ask, the more you will get. You will never get anything if you never dare to ask anything from this universe.

You are a part of this universe; whatever you do in your life, everything reflects back to you. The whole universe is always available for you. You are never alone in this universe. The blessing hands of this universe are always with you. You will always find someone close to you, for instance, your parents, your spouse, your siblings, your friends, and your fellow mates. They all are your universe. Trust them as you trust yourself.

When you smile, this universe will smile with you.

When you weep, this universe will weep with you.

When you succeed in your goal, this universe will rejoice with you. This universe is the first one to praise you and to be overwhelmed by your great achievements.

When you talk to yourself, this universe will listen to you first.

The energy, force, and power that are stored within you have been inherited from this universe.

Your happiness, your success, your peace, and your prosperity are all part of this universe.

The whole universe is within you; you just have to look inside yourself.

Only you can create your own universe.

Trust yourself before you trust anybody in your life.

Trusting yourself means you trust this universe.

With your trust, you can create your own universe.

4. Look for the Silver Lining

Behind the casting of dark clouds, there is always a sparkling ray of sunlight.

This whole world is like a big sea, and your life is like a small boat sailing on it in search of your last shore. Throughout this long voyage of your life, you will encounter numerous tempests, thunderstorms, and high and low tides. But you have to keep your silver lining alive and sail your small boat persistently until you touch the ultimate shore of your life.

The voyage of Columbus was not easy when he set out to discover the new land, 'America.' He went through countless challenges and upheavals on his unknown voyage. Many of his crew members died due to unseen diseases, hunger, and thirst in the middle of the journey. At one stage, the situation escalated, and his own crew members threatened to kill him if he wouldn't halt the voyage.

But Columbus didn't give up his mission to discover the new land. He ignited a silver lining at every juncture of his voyage, and at the same time, he showed new rays of hope to his crew members. Finally, he discovered the new land, 'America.'

During the British rule in India, many thousands of Indian freedom fighters were imprisoned in the dark and perilous cellular jail in Kalapani (situated in the Andaman and Nicobar Islands). They were harshly tortured by the British rulers and jailers and kept in inhumane conditions. But they tolerated the barbaric acts and malicious conduct of the British officers and jailers with their smiling faces, keeping their silver lining alive. They knew that one day their motherland would be liberated from British colonial power. They kindled their silver lining in every dark hour of their lives. They enlightened their minds, hearts, and souls with vivid optimism. And finally, they witnessed the freedom of their motherland from the foreign yoke in the year 1947 (India gained her independence).

We all are alive in this world because our hopes are alive.

Without hope, we can't live our life for a second.

It is your hope that helps you to peep into your future.

If there is hope, there is life.

Always see the silver lining in every tough situation in your life. It gives you strength, energy, and power to tackle every tough situation.

It gives you enough courage, self-belief, and self-confidence. It makes you devoted and patient to hold everything in your hands.

Never kill your high spirit and high optimism.

Never give up in your life, no matter how much a difficult situation will try to knock you down; move ahead in the mission of your life, and keep your silver lining in front of your view.

After every dark night, there is a dawn.

You will always see the glorious sunlight.

Keep your silver lining alive at every juncture of your life.

You will find the destiny of your life very close to you.

Always see the silver lining in every tough situation in your life.

It gives you strength, energy, and power to tackle every tough situation.

5. Celebrate Life

Grow your life every day and celebrate its beauty and fragrance.

Make your life beautiful with your good causes and noble deeds.

Love yourself and give your love to everyone.

Be happy and celebrate your happiness with heart and soul.

Forget your past and delete your bad memories and experiences, and move on.

Life means going ahead, but never turning your back.

Accept the hardships and failures of your life with open arms. Treat them as the stepping stones to your great fortune and success.

Make friends with everyone, but never make enemies with anyone. You will never gain anything through animosity.

Maintain a good rapport with everyone. It brings you closer to all.

Give up your bad thoughts and bad habits. Your bad thoughts will pollute your mind, and your bad habits will ruin your beautiful life.

Always open the door of self-improvement and self-development for yourself, and amend yourself every day. Bring good thoughts and good ideas into your life. There is great power in your thoughts and ideas. One good thought and one good idea may change your life.

Bring positive energy into your life, and drive away negative energy from your life. Your positive energy is like a life-saving potion, but your negative energy is like a poisonous dose.

Your positive energy consists of your good thoughts, good ideas, and good actions. Your negative energy consists of your bad thoughts, bad ideas, and bad actions.

Try to create something new in your life every day and make your life meaningful and purposeful.

Make your world like a beautiful garden where you can enjoy your life forever.

Give up your egos, angers, anxieties, attachments, hatreds, and greed. These are the biggest enemies of your life that steal your happiness and peace.

Fill your life with the flavors of love, happiness, compassion, kindness, peace, and prosperity.

Love your work like you love your loved ones. Worship your work like a priest worships God. Give your one hundred percent effort and dedication to your work.

Always keep your good health. There is no use for your wealth if you have bad health. Your biggest wealth is your good health.

Don't blame or criticize anyone. Instead, be a well-wisher to everyone.

Try to be your own critic and encourage yourself.

Make good plans and prepare yourself every day. Set the mission of your life and follow it until you reach its final destiny.

Always follow the golden rule of life: simple living and high thinking.

Be content with yourself, whatever you do and earn in your life. But never regret. You will always be happy and content in your entire life.

There is great beauty in simplicity. Make your life simple.

Never try to make your life complex.

Concentrate and do simple and small things first. Then follow with the next big things.

First of all, break complex things into compound things, and then break compound things into simple things.

Complex Things → Compound Things → Simple Things

You will never live your life with complex and compound things; you will only live your life with simple things.

Balance and adjust yourself in every situation of your life, both in good times and in bad times.

Always be flexible in your life.

Balance your family life as well as your professional life equally. Spend quality time with your loved ones, family members, and friends. It will multiply your joy and happiness in your life.

Celebrate your life with every little thing. But don't wait for the big things in order to celebrate your life. Every little celebration makes you happy and brings happiness, prosperity, and peace into your life.

Don't wait for any occasion to celebrate your life. Nobody knows what will happen next. Life is very unpredictable. Life is always short and a mystery. Don't postpone the celebration of your life for the next day; enjoy and celebrate your life every day.

Celebrate every moment of your life, and make every moment special and memorable.

Celebrate your life every day.

Celebrate your life with every little thing.

Every little celebration makes you happy and brings happiness, prosperity, and peace to your life.

6. Positive view

If you take a positive view in your life, you will always see possibility in everything. Your positive view will show you the possible way in every impossible thing. It will enlighten your mind to use your ideas and logic to tackle every impossible task.

If you take a positive view in your life, you will find the good side in everything. Your positive view will open your inner eyes to peep into the good side of everything. There are always two sides to everything: the good side and the bad side. Your positive view will always guide you toward the good side.

If you take a positive view in your life, you will find solutions to every problem. Your positive view will help you use the right tactics to approach every problem. It will solve every problem in an effortless manner. Your positive view is the only way to handle every problem in your life.

If you take a positive view in your life, you will see new ways and new directions. Your positive view will unveil every mystery of your life. It will direct you to choose the right key and unbolt the new doors of your opportunities. If you take a positive view in your life, you will be able to maintain yourself, and you can bring order and discipline to your life. You will know what is significant for you and what is insignificant. It will help you judge yourself in the right ways and the right manner.

If you take a positive view in your life, you will never get disappointed. Your positive view will help you become practical in your life. You will know the essential parts of your life and the unessential parts of your life. You will easily counteract yourself in every up and down of your life. You will never become emotional in your life, no matter what happens. You will never trap yourself in the cage of attachment. You will be able to manage yourself in both happiness and sorrow, in both success and failure. You will easily maintain your composure and equilibrium in your life.

If you take a positive view in your life, you can change and transform yourself. Your positive view will never allow you to be stagnant in your life. You will become flexible in your life. You will cope with the dynamics of life. You will maintain your stance in every circumstance of your life. Nothing will bother you. You will be able to adjust yourself in any place and anywhere in the world.

If you take a positive view in your life, you will be happy and content with yourself. You will find every reason to enjoy your life. You will know how to keep yourself happy and content in your life. In every harsh situation in your life, you will always discover some reason to keep your smile alive. Your positive view doesn't allow you to shed your precious tears unnecessarily.

If you take a positive view in your life, nobody can divert your mind. Nobody can move you away from your goal. You will become your own guide and mentor. You will know your right goal and its right direction. It keeps your self-belief and self-confidence alive and intact. It will lead you to your ultimate goal.

If you take a positive view in your life, you will always charge up in every approach. Your positive view will inject a dose of tremendous energy and power within you. It will help you know your true self. It will awaken your hidden potential. In every tough situation in your life, it will keep your mind, heart, and soul alive, boost you up, and give you a giant leap.

If you take a positive view in your life, you will definitely reach your goal. It is only your positive view that leads you at every stage of your life, whether you are in a state of happiness or in a state of sorrow; whether you are in a state of success or in a state of failure; whether you are alive or in a state of death.

Always take a positive view in your life; you will see possibility in everything.

You will never divert from your path in life.

You will always find the right direction in every puzzling situation.

7. Have some fun

Don't forget to smile.

Your smile is like a jewel of your life. Wear it every day. It is like a perfume that keeps you fresh and animated. Life is very short and precious. Don't waste your time on worthless things and events. Whatever time you get or can manage, make some fun and keep your smile and laughter alive. Your smile and laughter are the best antidotes to your worries and adversities.

Always choose happiness in your life.

Your happiness is the biggest asset of your life. You can't buy or borrow it from someone or anybody. It is a wealth that is always available within you; you just have to unearth it. Your happiness always keeps you energetic and enthusiastic.

Spend some quality time with your loved ones.

You can't live alone in this world. Your life is like a journey, and your loved ones are like your fellow travelers. You can only make your life enjoyable and memorable when you spend quality time together with them. You can't relish the true joy and happiness of your life until you spend quality time with your loved ones.

Enjoy yourself even if you are alone in your life.

Your life is a lone journey; you will never find everyone close to you all the time. Sometimes you will have to spend time alone. You will only realize the true importance of your happiness when you are alone. Even if you are alone in your life, don't forget to keep your joy and happiness alive.

Love yourself and love your beloved ones.

Love is the only way to live anywhere in this world. There is no other alternative to love. Love yourself like you love your girlfriend, boyfriend, or spouse. It is only your love that keeps you happy and alive. Your love is the mother of everything. Everything is possible with your love. Only your love brings you the magical charms in your life.

Forget your worries and enjoy your life.

Don't worry about anything; just enjoy your life, whatever the situation may be. Whatever is destined to happen will happen. You will never stop it. It is not in your hands. Your worries will only steal your energy and power. Your worries will make you weak and fatigued. They will kill your self-belief and self-confidence. Block it. Remove it. Don't allow it to enter your life. Forget it and replace it with your joy, happiness, and enthusiasm. In its place, think, contemplate, and act, and choose the right path to reach your goal.

Forget your setbacks and failures of yesterday and the past.

The best way to move ahead in your life is to forget whatever setbacks and failures you have faced in your past. The remembrance of your past setbacks and failures only brings you worries and regrets. You will never get anything from your past setbacks and failures. It is useless to relive your past setbacks and failures. It is just a waste of your precious time. Instead of recollecting your past happenings, it is better to think and act with a fresh mind and work with new plans.

Plan something new every day.

Don't waste your valuable time on worthless things. Make new plans every day and execute them with a positive approach. If your first plan doesn't work, then make another new plan; yet again, if your second plan doesn't work, then make your third plan, and so forth. Make your plans until they don't work for you. Even if possible, make one thousand new plans. Out of these one thousand plans, at least one plan will definitely work for you one hundred percent. But don't leave your mind without making any plans.

Mould and improve your life and move ahead.

Like an artist molds and improves his art every day, you can also mold and improve yourself every day. It will give you new heights of excellence and greatness in your life. You will change and transform yourself. You will be reborn in your life. You will reinvent yourself.

Make every moment memorable and special.

The best way to live your life is to make every moment memorable and special. You can make every moment memorable and special when you love yourself and your loved ones unconditionally.

Don't forget to have some fun in your life.

Don't make your life dull and lifeless.

You will never live your life in a lifeless ambiance.

Make your life like the spring season, even in the midst of the autumn season of your life.

8. Count Each Day

Think every day.

Shape and clothe your mind with new thoughts and new ideas every day. Spread the wings of constructive and innovative thoughts and ideas in your life. There is great power in your thoughts and ideas. Your one thought can change your life. Your one idea can transform your world. Let your thoughts and ideas shape and clothe your life and lead you to the door of new opportunities.

Dream every day.

There is great power in your dreams. As you see yourself in your dreams, you realize yourself in your reality. Your dream is the replica of your reality. Your real world wouldn't be possible without your dream. Your dream is like a bone that is hidden in the flesh of your reality.

If you don't see a dream in your life, you won't achieve anything in your reality. Your dream is the diagram of your reality. Draw your dream every day and every night until it shapes into the foundation of your reality.

Plan every day.

Nothing is possible without making a plan in your life. Your success and failure both depend on how you plan. No plan, no work. And no work, no success. Be a good planner in your life.

Many people fail in their lives not because they lack talent and skills, but because they never plan anything. They move about randomly without making any plans. Their philosophy is, "Let's see what will happen." They gamble with their own lives.

Don't allow your life to move in an unplanned manner; you will reach nowhere. Without a plan, your life will revolve like a top, with no direction and no destiny. Only your plan leads you in the right direction in your life.

Make your right decision every day.

Your decision is very crucial for your life. Your one right decision will build your life. Your one wrong decision will ruin your life. Make your right decision with your right knowledge and experience.

Think and act like an experienced judge before you make any decision in your life. Never make any decision in a hurry. Never make any decision with your eyes blindfolded. Never make any decision with your emotional heart. Make your decision when you are confident and comfortable with yourself. Always make your decision wisely and intelligently.

Grow and develop yourself every day.

Be like a plant. Grow and develop yourself every day. Whatever you hear that is worthwhile and learn wisdom and knowledge, utilize and practice it in your life in order to grow and develop yourself. Don't waste anything in your life.

Prepare yourself every day.

Life is like a battle. Every moment, you have to prepare yourself. Your life is a big mystery. You never know what will happen next. You have to prepare yourself every moment.

Be like a vigilant and disciplined soldier. Prepare yourself every moment and every day. Prepare your mind, heart, and soul with powerful thoughts, ideas, wisdom, knowledge, experiences, skills, and talents. Nobody can defeat you in the battle of your life if you prepare yourself every moment and every day.

Set your target every day.

Be like a hunter. Always keep your target in front of your eyes. Don't move ahead without setting any target in your life. If you want to achieve something great in your life, then set your target every day and try to fulfill it by hook or by crook. Don't be afraid to set your target, whether it is tough, challenging, or impossible. Just set your target and chase it. Nobody will dare to stop you from hitting its bull's eye.

A rocket will never launch if it doesn't get proper elevation and a target. In a similar way, you couldn't launch your life at the summit of great success and glory without a proper target.

Only a man with a target will rule in this world. Without a proper target, your life will become directionless and remain standstill.

Don't procrastinate anything.

Life is very precious. Don't procrastinate anything that you can do today. Never leave anything for tomorrow. Tomorrow never comes in your life. Only today is in your hands. Do whatever you want to do today. Make your today successful and fruitful. Live your day fully like it is the last day of your life. Make your day remarkable and leave your legacy.

Do what is important for you.

Every moment is important for your life. Analyze and judge for yourself what is important to you and what is unimportant. The top priority in your life is to do your important work, not the unimportant work.

Every day counts in your life.

Every moment and every day counts in your life. Whatever you do today will count in your life. Even if you do nothing today, it will also count in your life. Nothing goes to waste. Everything counts in your life. Everything has its worth.

Always do something worthwhile in your life. Even if you are unable to do something physically, think and plan so that you can execute your thoughts, ideas, and plans into action later on.

Thinking and planning something also counts as doing something. But don't waste your time by doing nothing. You will never be rewarded if you don't do anything in your life. You will only be rewarded if you do something in your life.

Every day is important in your life. Every day is a golden day for you.

Once you miss your golden day, you will miss it forever…

Don't misuse it.

Do something great and special in your life.

Always remember that every day counts in your life.

9. Encouragement

Encourage and motivate yourself.

Don't wait for anyone or anybody to encourage and motivate you. Encourage and motivate yourself. Be your own encourager and motivator. Be self-dependent and self-reliant. Never depend on anyone or anybody. Be the liberator of your own weaknesses and shortcomings. Dig out your own energy and strength. Execute your own action plans and innovative ideas in your own growth and development. Drive the engine of your own life. Even if you fail to drive it, push yourself till the last breath of your life, but never give up in the middle of the crossroads of your life. Quench your own thirst if you ever can't find water to soothe it.

Don't wait for anybody.

Only a weak person waits for everybody. But a strong and powerful person never waits for anybody. He acts straight away in every move. Waiting for someone means you are relying on him. Don't rely on anybody if you want to reach your ultimate goal in life.

The bitter truth of life is that nobody waits for anybody. Everybody has their own aims and objectives. Nobody has time to wait for you. If you wait for anybody, then you will be lagging behind him, sooner or later. Therefore, whatever you want to do, do it right now, but don't wait for anybody. Wherever you want to go, go right now, but don't wait for anybody.

Be a learner.

Learning is a never-ending process. Every time, you can learn something. You have learned something right from your birth until now. There is no stoppage to your learning. You can learn something from everywhere.

There are infinite things to learn in your life. You can't complete your learning in this lifetime. Nobody can claim that he or she has learned everything in this world. There is an abundance of things to learn in your life.

There is great beauty in learning new things. Don't stop your learning. There is no age limit to learning something. You can learn from everybody and from everywhere. There is no limit to learning. Learning is an art. Cultivate this art of learning in your life.

Learn something worthwhile every day so that you can utilize it in your day-to-day life.

Teach yourself every day.

Don't wait for anyone or anybody to teach you everything in your life. Know yourself. Discover yourself. Observe. Read. Write. Learn. Listen. Speak. And then teach yourself. Whatever good things you find in your life, learn from them and teach yourself.

Guide yourself.

If you don't find your guide or mentor in your life, then don't wait for anyone. Start guiding yourself. Use your common sense and follow your conscience and intuition, and then guide yourself. You will always find the right direction in your life.

Be the master of your own.

Whatever field or career you choose in your life, master it yourself before you step into it. Prepare yourself. Train yourself. Test yourself. Experiment on yourself. Discover yourself. Then act like a master. When you become the master in your chosen field or career, nobody can defeat you. You will always be a winner in your chosen field or career.

Lead your own life.

Lead your own life like a leader. Life is yours, and it is your sole responsibility to lead your own life. If you can't lead your life, then nobody can lead you. You will become directionless. You will wander in your own life like a wayfarer.

The hidden ability of your leadership is within you. You just need to awaken your leadership qualities. You are the best leader of your own life. Nobody can lead you better than you yourself because you know yourself better than anybody else.

Learn from your own experience.

Your experience is the greatest teacher of your life. Learn from it and amend yourself. Your experience of life never goes to waste. Only your experience makes you wise and mature in your life. Your experience of life is the biggest gain in your life.

You will never feel the real joy and happiness of your grand success and glory if you never gain the experiences of your bitter failures and hardships.

You will only manage yourself if you have experiences from your life.

Think and act like a winner.

If you assume your life is a game, then play your game like a winner. Give your heart and soul to your game. Never allow anyone to take over your winning seat or trophy. Prepare yourself in such a manner that nobody can stand before you. Make yourself so powerful and mighty that nobody can ever dare to defeat you.

Defeat your own competitor.

You are the biggest competitor in your own life. Nobody can defeat you in your life without your consent. But it is only you who can defeat you.

Your weaknesses defeat you. Your worries defeat you. Your inferiority complex defeats you. Your self-doubts defeat you. Your wrong ideas defeat you. Your wrong plans defeat you. Your wrong decisions defeat you. Your wrong executions defeat you. Your wrong actions defeat you. Your wrong timing and wrong moves defeat you.

You never blame anyone or anything for your own defeat; you have to blame yourself. You are responsible for your own defeat.

Look at yourself in the mirror whenever you feel defeated in your life; you will see yourself as the biggest competitor in your own life.

Become like a fighter.

You will never achieve or gain anything in this world without fighting. This whole world is like a battlefield. This world is for fighters, not for quitters.

You are always surrounded by tough challenges and opponents everywhere. You have to prepare yourself every moment.

You will never get anything with your prayers and pleas in this world. You have to fight for whatever you want in your life. Nobody will give you a single penny or a piece of bread for free. You have to earn it and pay the price for whatever you want.

Plan yourself like a fighter.

Train yourself like a fighter.

Fight like a fighter.

Win like a fighter.

Live like a fighter.

And die like a fighter.

Always remember that only a fighter can live in this world with pride and dignity.

Encourage yourself day and night until you receive the sparkling energy and power of your courage and high spirit.

If you don't find encouragement from anyone in your life, then encourage yourself...

10. Appreciation

Appreciate your good thoughts.

You are made of your own thoughts. If your thoughts are good, you will become good in your life. On the other hand, if your thoughts are bad, you will become bad in your life. Your good thoughts always lead you to the right paths, while your bad thoughts always lead you to the wrong paths.

Your thoughts are the seeds of your actions. Your thoughts are the driving force behind your actions. The way you sow your thoughts determines the way you grow in your life and the way you become in your life.

Your good thoughts are the first signs of your good nature. They will enrich your life and build your world. Therefore, polish and mold your thoughts every day.

Appreciate your good dreams.

Love your dreams and believe in your dreams; at the same time, never forget to appreciate your good dreams. Your dreams are the true dimension of your realities. It is only your dreams that shape your life and your world. You are alive in this world because you know how to see your dreams. But if you don't know how to see your dreams, the very moment you will die. Your beautiful world will disappear from your eyesight. You will live like a living corpse.

Appreciate your good imaginations.

There is great power in your imagination. You can imagine anything in your life. It is like a blueprint of your reality.

If you can imagine, then only can you make anything in your life. If you can imagine anything, then only can you create something new in your life. If you can imagine something, then only can you build something great in your life.

An architect imagines the design of a building before he actually draws it on a sheet of paper. Without imagination, he couldn't design anything.

Without imagination, nobody can do anything in life.

Appreciate your good ideas.

Your good ideas are the life changers and game changers in your life. With your good ideas, you can change and transform the course of your life. Your good ideas are the keys to unlocking your hidden potential.

Many big things are done and created only because of one good idea. Many big industries are set up only because of one good idea. Many big discoveries and inventions are made only because of one good idea. Behind every great success, there is the role of one good idea.

Appreciate your good plans.

Your good plan is the driving force of your success. Without making a good plan, you will never approach anything in your life. Your good plan is the roadmap to your success.

Your good plan gives you a clear vision and mission in your life. Your good plan directs you on how to execute anything in your life. Without making a good plan, you will always lose in your life.

To achieve anything in your life, you have to make good plans. To win anything in your life, you have to make good plans.

Appreciate your good decisions.

Your good decisions always lead you to your ultimate goal. Before you make any decision in your life, always read, learn, observe, analyze, and judge everything with your clear vision.

Never make any decision in your life with your emotional heart and under the influence of someone or anybody. Your decision will go one hundred percent wrong. Make your own decision with your logical mind.

Your decision is very crucial for you because it will decide your entire life. One right decision may lead you to the road of success and glory, and one wrong decision may lead you to the ditch of downfall.

Appreciate your good preparation.

Your life is like a big examination. Every moment and every day is a new examination for you. You are like an examinee, and the challenges and upheavals ahead of you are your examiners.

You couldn't clear the examinations of your life without proper preparation. You have to prepare yourself every second, every minute, every hour, every day, every week, every month, and every year.

You never know what challenges and upheavals are eagerly waiting for you. You have to prepare yourself mentally, physically, and spiritually. You have to prepare yourself like a great warrior.

Appreciate your good actions.

Your actions speak louder than your words. Mind your actions before you actually act. It is only your actions that rule your life. No word has ever ruled your life. Speak less and act more.

Your action is the only tool that will help you explore your hidden potential. Your action is the ultimate source of your success and glory. No action, no work; no result.

Appreciate yourself.

Nobody can appreciate you better than you can. Only you can appreciate yourself the best. Forget about others; forget what they will say about you. You will never stop the barking dogs. It is the nature of a dog to bark for no reason.

Appreciate yourself even if you are not good. Appreciate yourself even if you can't believe you are the best, but with time you will believe you are the best. But never discourage yourself for any reason.

Never ever blame yourself for any reason. Never ever regret yourself for any reason. Whatever is going to happen will happen whether you want it to or not. You can't stop it. Instead of blaming yourself, figure out your weak points and amend them straightaway. Self-blaming means you are discouraging yourself for no reason.

Happiness and sorrow, success and failure, are the never-ending cycles of your life. They will always happen in your life like day and night. Nobody can stop it. If you rise today, then tomorrow you will fall down, and vice versa. This is the law of nature. You have to accept it.

Always appreciate yourself no matter what happens in your life. It will boost your energy level and help you bounce back in your life after every downfall.

Appreciate yourself whenever you do anything good in your life.

Don't expect any appreciation from anybody.

Appreciate yourself.

Nobody can appreciate you better than you can.

About the author:

Birister Sharma is a full time author. He is also an avid reader. He loves reading, writing, and motivation. He has penned down dozens of self-help motivational books and novels so far.

You may contact him @ birister2007@gmail.com